PRODUCTS: FROM IDEA TO MARKET

Sneakers

by Abby Doty

www.focusreaders.com

Copyright © 2025 by Focus Readers®, Mendota Heights, MN 55120. All rights reserved. No part of this book may be reproduced or utilized in any form or by any means without written permission from the publisher.

Focus Readers is distributed by North Star Editions:
sales@northstareditions.com | 888-417-0195

Produced for Focus Readers by Red Line Editorial.

Photographs ©: iStockphoto, cover, 1, 6, 13, 16, 25, 26; Shutterstock Images, 4, 8, 11, 15, 19, 20, 22, 29

Library of Congress Cataloging-in-Publication Data
Library of Congress Cataloging-in-Publication Data is available on the Library of Congress website.

ISBN
979-8-88998-406-1 (hardcover)
979-8-88998-434-4 (paperback)
979-8-88998-487-0 (ebook pdf)
979-8-88998-462-7 (hosted ebook)

Printed in the United States of America
Mankato, MN
012025

About the Author

Abby Doty is a writer, editor, and booklover from Minnesota.

Table of Contents

CHAPTER 1
New Sneakers 5

CHAPTER 2
Sketching Sneakers 9

THAT'S AMAZING!
Air Jordans 14

CHAPTER 3
Making Sneakers 17

CHAPTER 4
Factories to Feet 23

Focus Questions • 28

Glossary • 30

To Learn More • 31

Index • 32

CHAPTER 1

New Sneakers

A girl watches TV at home. A sneaker **commercial** comes on. It shows a woman running in new sneakers. She moves quickly. The shoes look bright and colorful.

Sneaker commercials often show people in action.

Some sneakers are made for tracks and pavement. Others are great for basketball courts.

The girl has sneakers already. But they make her feet hurt. So, she buys the sneakers from the commercial. They feel light and strong. They bend well, too.

The girl goes to a running track. She puts on the new sneakers and ties the laces. The shoes feel comfortable. Then, the girl begins running around the track. The shoes support her feet. They help her move faster. She is amazed. She wonders how someone created these sneakers.

Did You Know?
Wearing shoes that don't fit right can change how a person moves.

CHAPTER 2
Sketching Sneakers

Shoe companies do a lot of work before making new sneakers. First, companies think about their future customers. They choose who to make shoes for. Some companies only make sneakers for athletes.

Many shoe stores have sections just for different types of sneakers.

Others create sneakers for kids. These categories help companies choose general ideas.

Next, companies create **designs** for new sneakers. To do this, companies may look at **trends**. In one year, high-top sneakers may be popular. In another year, people may buy lots of chunky, colorful sneakers.

Companies often try to take part in trends. But in other cases, companies may decide to avoid

People may want to buy shoes that are similar to what their friends have.

trends. That can help their shoes stand out from the crowd.

Companies choose materials as they design. They may want to try out new materials. For example, a design might use a new fabric that is strong but light.

When the designs are ready, companies make **prototypes**. To do this, workers use tools called lasts. Lasts are model feet. They help shape the shoe.

After that, companies test their prototypes. Sneakers must be comfortable and durable. So, testers make sure the sneakers

Did You Know?

Completing a sneaker design can take more than a year.

> Some designers use computer tools to help them figure out the measurements and look of the shoes.

won't break. They walk and run in the shoes. They give their opinions. Companies use those ideas. Then they make changes. Workers keep trying until the designs are perfect.

THAT'S AMAZING!

Air Jordans

Air Jordans first came out in 1985. Nike created the shoes for basketball star Michael Jordan. The sneakers were different from other shoes at the time. Air Jordans had bold colors. They worked well on the basketball court. But they also looked good off the court.

Customers loved Air Jordans right away. They became the best-selling sneakers of all time. The shoes also brought a wider change. They helped sneakers become a bigger part of Black culture. Since then, Black culture has **influenced** sneaker design and popularity.

 Nike has released many different versions of Air Jordans.

CHAPTER 3

Making Sneakers

When designs are ready, shoe companies make lots of their sneakers. This usually happens in factories. Many factories start with the sole. This is the bottom of the shoe. Workers make a mold.

Sneaker soles often include rubber and foam.

This piece is made in the shape of the shoe. Workers melt materials into the mold. Then the sole cools and hardens.

Factories also make the top parts of shoes. Uppers are often made of fabric, leather, or mesh. They can use **synthetic** materials. To make the upper, workers use tools called dies. Dies work like cookie cutters. They cut out pieces of fabric. First, a die goes over the material. Next, a machine presses down on the die.

Workers check each piece as it is made.

It cuts out the shape. Then the fabric moves to other machines. These machines sew the pieces together. When the upper is done, it goes onto a last.

19

▷ **Adding details such as shoelaces often happens at the end of production.**

After that, it is time to connect the sole and upper. In some cases, workers heat the two parts. Or they may spread glue on them. Then workers connect the pieces.

Machines press down. They make sure the pieces stick together.

The shoe is almost done. Workers take the sneaker off the last. They add final touches and check for mistakes. Finally, workers pack all the sneakers. They send the shoes to stores. The sneakers are ready for customers to buy.

Did You Know?

One sneaker can have more than 50 different pieces.

CHAPTER 4
Factories to Feet

When sneakers reach stores, shoe companies are still not done. They need people to notice and buy their shoes. So, they **advertise** to buyers. Companies may use famous people to do this.

Many sneaker ads show people running or playing sports.

23

Celebrities can talk about the sneakers' style or feel. Athletes appear in sneaker ads, too. They can show how sneakers help them. Ads may show them winning games. These appearances can make customers more likely to buy.

Ads also tell buyers the best details about new sneakers. Some buyers want shoes for sports. Others want sneakers to wear at work and at home. So, companies show those features to buyers.

Some sneaker ads feature hiking or nature scenes.

They let customers know what their sneakers can do.

Companies also remind buyers of their other **products**. That is because some people stick to the same brands. They buy from companies they enjoyed before.

Choosing specific colors is a common way to customize sneakers.

Many companies use social media to communicate with people. Buyers may enjoy hearing the story behind a sneaker's design. Companies can share these stories directly with buyers.

In other cases, businesses let people **customize** sneakers. That gives customers a personal connection to the shoe.

In the end, the ads help customers find sneakers that are perfect for them. The shoes came a long way to reach their feet.

Did You Know?

Some companies sell limited-time sneakers. People often want to buy the shoes before they're gone.

Focus Questions

Write your answers on a separate piece of paper.

1. Write a few sentences explaining how companies advertise sneakers.

2. What feature of sneakers do you think is most useful? Why?

3. What is a last?
   - **A.** a brand-new shoe
   - **B.** a model foot
   - **C.** a tool to cut shapes

4. Why might customers buy sneakers that a celebrity advertises?
   - **A.** Customers may trust the celebrity's opinion.
   - **B.** Customers think the celebrity's ads are boring.
   - **C.** Customers forget to buy shoes when they see the celebrity.

5. What does **durable** mean in this book?

*Sneakers must be comfortable and **durable**. So, testers make sure the sneakers won't break. They walk and run in the shoes.*

    A. weak and small
    B. tough and long-lasting
    C. large and thin

6. What does **limited-time** mean in this book?

*Some companies sell **limited-time** sneakers. People often want to buy the shoes before they're gone.*

    A. sold forever
    B. never made or sold
    C. sold during a short period

Answer key on page 32.

Glossary

advertise
To make messages or videos about a product so customers want to buy it.

commercial
A message or video to sell a product. It appears during other programs.

customize
To change details of a product for a certain person.

designs
Plans that include the size, materials, and shape of a product.

influenced
Affected what people did, thought, or created.

products
Items that are for sale.

prototypes
Early forms of something, usually for testing.

synthetic
Made by people, not by nature.

trends
Things that are popular for a period of time.

To Learn More

BOOKS

Green, Sara. *Nike*. Minneapolis: Bellwether Media, 2024.

Hill, Christina. *Supply Chains in Infographics*. Ann Arbor, MI: Cherry Lake Press, 2023.

Respicio, Mae. *The Story of Sneakers*. North Mankato, MN: Capstone Press, 2025.

NOTE TO EDUCATORS

Visit **www.focusreaders.com** to find lesson plans, activities, links, and other resources related to this title.

Index

A
advertising, 23–24, 27
Air Jordans, 14
athletes, 9, 24

B
Black culture, 14

C
celebrities, 23–24
commercials, 5–6
customizing, 27

D
design, 10–13, 14, 17, 26
dies, 18–19

F
factories, 17–18

J
Jordan, Michael, 14

L
lasts, 12, 19, 21

M
materials, 11, 18,

P
products, 25
prototypes, 12

S
social media, 26
soles, 17–18, 20
synthetic materials, 18

T
testers, 12–13
trends, 10–11

U
uppers, 18–20